Explaining
Defensive Spiritual
Warfare

Tom Marshall

Sovereign World

Bible quotations are taken from
The Holy Bible, New International Version.
© copyright 1973, 1978, 1984 International Bible Society.
Used by permission.

New King James Version of the Bible
© copyright 1983 Thomas Nelson Inc,
Box 141000, Nashville, TN 37214, USA.

Revised Standard Version of the Bible
© copyright 1946, 1952 by The Division of Christian Education of
the National Council of Churches of Christ in the United States of America.

American Standard Bible © copyright The Lockman Foundation, USA.

ISBN: 1 85240 156 7

SOVEREIGN WORLD LIMITED
P.O. Box 777, Tonbridge, Kent TN11 9XT, England.

Typeset and printed in the UK by Sussex Litho Ltd, Chichester, West Sussex.

Publisher's Preface

The following booklet has been compiled from several tape recordings of talks Tom Marshall gave just weeks before his unexpected death.

Tom was planning to write a book on Spiritual Warfare for us, however this was not to be. We therefore pray that this little booklet will convey to you some of his thoughts and be a great blessing and strength to you. We know that would be his wish.

Contents

Introduction

In this booklet I want to share with you the issue of defensive spiritual warfare. I believe this is one of the most exciting yet crucial issues that faces the Church today.

I became aware some time ago, that there are a number of Christians and churches who are going through very difficult times in these days. They have got hold of the idea of spiritual warfare, galloped into battle, and then been suddenly flattened and they don't know why. I believe the reason is they have not learned how to defend themselves in a war. It is something they don't understand.

The Psalmist says that it is God *"who trains my hands for war, my fingers for battle"* (Psalm 144:1). God trains us for battle. If we get into spiritual warfare and we are untrained in the principles and issues facing us, we will be flattened if we are not careful.

So I want to deal with the whole issue of how spiritual warfare impacts our personal and corporate life, and what is involved in defending them.

1

Recognising a
Spiritual Attack

I want to start by making the point that in the troubles and difficulties we go through from time to time as Christians, we need to distinguish very carefully what is a spiritual attack from either:

a. The inevitable consequences that follow on our disobedience or our violation of the principles of Scripture, or

b. The circumstances that are permitted by the Holy Spirit as character building exercises or growth lessons in faith.

a. We have to be careful not to expect demons to 'pop out of the woodwork' every time we come against something difficult in our lives, or we will always be telling people we are under attack and having such a terrible time! You may be – or you may not be, for to be honest, one of the reasons we often face problems as Christians, is because we are actually violating God's principles, or neglecting the instruction of God's Word. If you don't behave correctly in those areas then your Christian life is going to come unstuck, so it won't be spiritual warfare at all.

In fact the devil does not need to bother with us when that happens. I think that one of the things the devil does is to tempt Christians so that when we fall, when we disobey God by neglecting his principles, Satan can just walk off and leave us to carry the consequences of our misdeeds. That is not spiritual warfare.

b. There are certain difficult circumstances that we go through that are actually meant to be training exercises. God wants them to produce character in us. They are meant to produce some stamina and backbone in our Christian life. I would encourage you, particularly those who would claim to be charismatic Christians, to spend quite a bit of time reading Paul's second letter to the church at Corinth. When you do, you will be surprised to find that Paul says things like this... *"I was depressed; I was scared; I was afraid; I was so pressured I thought I was going to die."* This was Paul, the great and mighty apostle. It amazes me how frank Paul is with the stresses he goes through as a believer.

When we go through those stresses, we need to understand God's purpose is that they are meant to be training exercises for us. I used to preach a message called 'The Gospel of Suffering' but people today don't want to listen to 'The Gospel of Suffering', so I called it 'Biblical Stress Management'! It's the same thing.

The church that Paul wrote to so frankly wasn't the magisterial Church of Rome; it wasn't his favourite church of Philippi; it wasn't the wonderful revelational church of Ephesus; it was the church at Corinth. That bunch of crazy charismatics that took Paul all his time to keep on track! This was the church he opened his mind to about his problems. He understood it was not spiritual warfare.

Summary

We must distinguish what is really spiritual attack from either:

a. The inevitable consequences that follow our disobedience or our violation of the principles of Scripture, or

b. The circumstances that are permitted by the Holy Spirit as character building exercises or growth lessons in faith.

2

Why Christians Come Under Spiritual Attack

Spiritual warfare, or attack, is liable to happen to us in the following circumstances. It is important that we understand why.

1. We are a threat to the devil's position or his possessions

If in our life, in our faith, or in our behaviour individually or corporately the devil thinks that we are threatening his possessions or his position, he will attack. He has learned that the best means of defence is attack and so he will react. Those of you in business are, I am sure, often aware of what I mean. I want you to understand what happens.

A business or a corporation or a city, or for that matter a church, has an inner life that is actually spirit. We are spirit beings and when we corporately create an organisation there comes into being a corporate spirit. This thing is alive. This thing manages people, uses people, shapes people, controls people and dominates people. I remember speaking at a business seminar in Oxford, England, and a man came up to me afterwards and said "I am a senior manager in an oil company and what you are saying today is exactly right. I have to go to meetings of people from all different oil companies. I can walk into a room and within five minutes, without anybody telling me the company they belong to, I can pick them every time. They talk differently, their attitudes are different, they behave differently. They are stamped by their company life." When we are serving the business, serving the government department or whatever, we are aware of that.

This 'corporate spirit' is not only alive but it is fallen. It is not only fallen but it is idolatrous, and it has two main aims.

(a) It will do anything to **survive**. Many years ago in New Zealand, I remember seeing an interview on television with the then Prime Minister. The interviewer said to him "Mr. Prime Minister, what is the first principle of government?" Now you would think he would have said that the first principle of government is to govern, or the first principle of government is justice but he didn't say that. He said "the first principle of government is to stay in power." He would do anything to survive. A church will do anything to survive. A business will do anything to survive.

(b) The second thrust of a corporation is **idolatry**. In Isaiah 47:8 Babylon the City says this: *"I am,"* says Babylon, *"I am and there is none besides me. I will never be a widow or suffer the loss of children."* In contrast in Isaiah 45:18 & 21 God says *"I am... and there is no God apart from me."*

The corporation has this idolatrous drive that it wants to dominate people and be the ultimate authority of their lives.

I remember a man at that same seminar who said to me, "Last week I was at church during the week and my boss rang up. My wife said, 'Bill's not here but at a church meeting' and down the telephone came an annoyed voice saying, 'what on earth is he doing at a church meeting? – I want him at home doing his paperwork. He has got to be on the road in the morning.'"

What does that show? It shows an idolatrous drive in the business spirit that wants to rule. Whenever a Christian lives under a corporation like that, the corporation tries to impact the shape of the believer's life, and to establish its value standards and its ethical standards. It shows that this is the spirit that the employee has to obey. Sometimes those standards are non-Christian and even anti-Christian as far as you and I are concerned. We are aware of that impact.

We need to understand about the demonic powers whose aim is to manage and control the corporation and what is happening all the time. Some of the decisions made in boardrooms may be totally amoral as far as the Christian is concerned. What is driving those people? They are not necessarily evil men. They are being dominated by demonic powers and the same powers may well be trying to influence believers.

What is our protection? It is this. We are indwelt by the Holy Spirit and his presence in the believer's life can keep us free from that domination by a business power. We can live with the business, like Daniel, serve it legitimately because it can have legitimate ends, and do so without bending the knees, without allowing it to impose its moral standard upon us. But to be realistic we have to understand that if we are doing that, there will be antagonism from the corporation and antagonism from the demons. That is where we are liable to come under spiritual attack.

I have no doubt that many of you reading this will have been aware of an alien force, a non-Christian influence, in your workplace. You are most likely up against demonic powers. You threaten their position and authority because of the presence of the Holy Spirit within you.

2. Satan is probing for our weaknesses

It can happen to us because all the time the devil is probing for our weaknesses. He believes that every one of us has a place of 'battlefield vulnerability'. He wants to discover what that is and he will do anything to find it.

The devil believes that every one of us has our price. Every one of us has our breaking point. That is what he is after. This is the cause of much of the pressure we come under from time to time.

3. Satan is trying to neutralise and destroy us

More seriously, if the devil can neutralise us, then he will destroy us. This is his ultimate aim. It is vitally important that we understand that the war we are involved in is a real war. It is not make-believe. We are not playing games. The enemy wants to get us on our own and destroy us so he will try to isolate us: isolate us from God; isolate us from one another, isolate us from our friends, isolate us from our churches. When he has done this and we are on our own, he will seek to destroy us.

It is important to understand that most attacks come through people. Words will be said by people and things will be done by people. Actions will be taken by people. Bitterness will flow from the hearts of people. Remember, however, that people are never the enemy. The important thing to do when these things come upon us is to discern the real source of the attack, what it really is, so that we can deal with it. If you simply react to people you have lost the battle.

. Do you remember the time when Jesus was speaking to the disciples and asked them, *"Who do you say I am?"* and Peter said *"You are the Christ, the Son of the living God."* (Matthew 16:15, 16). It seems as if Jesus was so excited about that, he started to tell Peter he was going to go to Jerusalem, he was going to be crucified, he was going to be buried and he was going to rise again from the dead. What happened? Peter went straight up the wall! "That is never going to happen to you," he exclaimed. "Get rid of that, Lord, that's rubbish!" There was pressure on the spirit of Jesus. There was an attack coming at him. Somehow the enemy was trying to get him isolated from the Father's will and purpose for his life. Jesus discerned this and strongly rebuked Peter. *"Get thee behind me, Satan,"* he said. He wasn't having a go at Peter. The words came out of Peter's mouth but they originated from the devil.

We have to realise and remind ourselves all the time that, though people may be the vehicle of the attack, the person is never the enemy, I repeat, never the enemy. This is why sometimes you find that the devil can use Christians to attack other believers.

Summary

We are called to live in the power structures and to serve their legitimate ends but under the Lordship of Christ to refuse to:

a. Yield to the idolatrous spirit of the powers.

b. Take our moral standards or value system from the powers, and

c. allow the powers to be the ultimate authority in our life.

We must reckon realistically that from time to time we will come under attack from demonic powers.

Spiritual attack is the devil's attempt to deter us individually or corporately from pressing into battle and hitting targets. He understands that the best means of defence is attack.

a. He believes that we all have our price and our areas of vulnerability.

b. Satan is probing for our weaknesses.

c. The attacks can show us what weaknesses are sins, which calls for repentance and amendment.

What vulnerabilities call for protective strategies?
Alone or in relationships that we cannot trust we are vulnerable. Satan is trying to:

a. Isolate us from God and other believers.

b. Disable our defences.

Attack will most often come through people, **but remember people are never the enemy**. It takes real discernment to realise the true nature and source of the attack (Matthew 16:21-23).

3

Sources and Nature
of Demonic Attack

In this chapter I want to give you some situations where this kind of spiritual attack can happen. Below is a check list of circumstances which may occur in your personal life, your family life and your church life which are likely to be spiritual attacks from demonic powers.

Not every example given is necessarily evidence of demonic attack, but we need to recognise they may be.

1. Physical attacks
a. Sicknesses or physical conditions that have no medical reason or do not respond to medical treatment.
b. Attacks involving the appetites – eating disorders, food allergies, anorexia, alcoholism or drinking habits.
c. Sexual appetites, lust, sexual perversion, pornography, sexual disorders.
d. Nervous weaknesses and disorders, drug addictions.

2. Attacks on the mind
a. Compulsive or obsessive thoughts.
b. Ungovernable tongues given to criticism, slander and backbiting.
c. Confusion in thinking, extreme talkativeness or inability to communicate, extreme forgetfulness, fantasising, perplexity, overactive imagination.
d. Bad dreams, nightmares, insomnia or sleeplessness.
e. Indecision, indecisiveness, excessive procrastination, passivity.

3. Emotional attacks
a. Fears, worry, anxiety, dread.
b. Depression, moroseness, negativity.

c. Discouragement, hopelessness, despair.

d. Self doubt, condemnation, sense of failure.

e. Anger, aggressiveness, hostility, defensiveness.

4. Occult manifestations

a. Apparitions, visions.

b. Demonisation.

c. Psychic or mediumistic experiences or manifestations.

d. Self destructive or suicidal tendencies.

e. Effects of curses or maledictions.

5. Attacks based on personal sins

a. Bitterness, resentments, unforgiveness.

b. Rebellion against authority.

c. Pride and self-centredness.

d. Unconfessed and secret sins and self indulgences.

6. Attacks based on generational or ancestral sin

7. Abusive attacks

a. Domination, intimidation, control.

b. Sexual, emotional or verbal abuse.

c. Spiritual, psychological and other forms of abuse.

8. Attacks on marriages and families

a. Conflict, strife, breakdown in communication.

b. Sexual problems.

c. Parent/child behavioural problems.

d. Adulterous relationships or temptations.

9. Attacks on business and church life

a. Division and disunity.

b. Relational conflict, disloyalty, betrayal.

c. Personal attacks on character, ability, position or rights.

d. Rumour-mongering, gossip, character assassination.

e. Injustice, unfair treatment, persecution.

f. Financial and business pressures, unfair competition and opposition.

g. Pressure, stress and burn out.

10. Attacks on the spiritual life
a. Severe and irrational doubt, discouragement, lack of reality.
b. Resistance to prayer, Scripture and worship.
c. Deception, unbalance, false manifestations and cultic revelations.

I am not saying that everything I have listed always has a demonic source, but we need to be alert and check the source of the attack if any of the above things are around. It is clear just looking at the list to what extent our life can be interfered with and attacked by demonic powers.

4

Principles of Defensive Warfare

Now I want to give you some of the principles of defensive spiritual warfare for you to think about and study. We cannot over-emphasise the importance of defence, because the lack of secure defence leaves us open to surprise attack. This happens too frequently to Christians.

The devil will often try and rush our defences and overwhelm us. If our position is not secure, this will happen easily, and we will be bowled over before we know what has happened.

Occupy the High Ground

1   *He who dwells in the shelter of the Most High*
    will rest in the shadow of the Almighty.
2 *I will say of the Lord, "He is my refuge and my fortress,*
    my God, in whom I trust."
3 *Surely he will save you from the fowler's snare*
    and from the deadly pestilence.
4 *He will cover you with his feathers, and under his wings you*
        will find refuge;
    his faithfulness will be your shield and rampart.
5 *You will not fear the terror of night, nor the arrow that flies*
        by day,
6 *nor the pestilence that stalks in the darkness,*
    nor the plague that destroys at midday.
7 *A thousand may fall at your side, ten thousand at your right*
        hand, but it will not come near you.
8 *You will only observe with your eyes and see the punishment*
        of the wicked.

9   *If you make the Most High your dwelling –*
    Even the Lord, who is my refuge –
10 *then no harm will befall you, no disaster will come near*
        your tent.
11 *For he will command his angels concerning you to guard*
        you in all your ways;
12 *they will lift you up in their hands; so that you will not strike*
        your foot against a stone.
13 *You will tread upon the lion and the cobra;*
    you will trample the great lion and the serpent.
14 *"Because he loves me," says the Lord, "I will rescue him:*
    I will protect him, for he acknowledges my name.
15 *He will call upon me, and I will answer him;*
    I will be with him in trouble,
    I will deliver him and honour him.
16 *With long life will I satisfy him and show him my salvation."*

(Psalm 91:1-16)

This is an amazing psalm. David says it all so much better than I can!

The first principle of defensive warfare is to get onto the high ground. This is where you are safe, and where you can see what is happening. Battlefields are very confusing places where there is a lot of noise, a lot of smoke and a lot of things going on, and nobody knows what is happening. The devil will therefore try and get us down on to his ground where this kind of thing can affect us. The first and primary principle, therefore, of all defensive warfare is to get on to the high ground so that you can see what is going on from the beginning. This is where you are in touch with resources that will keep you safe and where your position is protected.

What is the high ground? Spiritually we have the high ground but in the secular city who has the high ground? If you look around the horizon of a city you will see who has! Have you ever wondered why those great gleaming skyscrapers are built – the banks, insurance companies, and multi-national companies? Do you understand that they are making a 'spiritual' statement? The Bible is full of references to high places. If you go into a pagan country and look around the hills you will find that the temples are built there on the high ground – they are making a statement. In a city those towers are making a spiritual statement. They are saying "here we have the power, here we have the resources, here we call the shots, here you bow to us." Their aim is to over-awe us with their power and cause us to bow the knee to them.

Recently I was in the City of Melbourne in Australia and there is a huge multi-storey office tower block being built right across the end of the main street there. It is the Head Office of one of the major brewers in the State of Victoria. When it is finished it will be difficult for anyone to go up the main street of that city without being confronted with this office block speaking about their brewery. There is a spiritual statement behind that. In the world the devil occupies the high ground so we need to know what our high ground is.

1. Our high ground is our revelational standing in Jesus Christ.
I recommend you to read the psalms of David. He was a man of war and knew the business of warfare. He is always speaking about "the Lord, my rock, my refuge, my high tower, my stronghold, my shield, my rampart." David knew what his high ground was.

"I love you, O Lord, my strength.
The Lord is my rock, my fortress, and my deliverer,
My God is my rock, in whom I take refuge.
He is my shield and the horn of my salvation,
my stronghold.
I call to the Lord who is worthy of praise
and I am saved from my enemies…" (Psalm 18:1-3)

David's psalms are full of these kinds of words. You would think by reading them however, that he was always running away from his enemies. Not so. Read the history and you will see that David was always running after his enemies! He knew where his stronghold, his safe place, his security was. He knew that the first principle of warfare was to get your defence secure. The first thing you need to know about battle is how to defend yourself

23

before you can learn how to attack the enemy. We need to be trained for battle. Psalm 18:32-34.

"It is God who arms me with strength and
makes my way perfect.
He makes my feet like the feet of a deer,
He enables me to stand on the heights.
He trains my hands for battle...."

God knows that we are in a war so he wants to train us for battle. The first principle of training is to get your defence secure and this is done by firstly knowing what your high ground is and your standing in Christ. **I am seated in heavenly places with God in Christ.** That is the Christian's security and high ground.

2. Our high ground is the victory of the death of Jesus Christ on the cross.

This is what the Bible means by the blood of Christ. The blood of Christ is a shorthand expression that sums up all the power, the awesome power, of the cross on our behalf. That's our high ground. I am seated in Christ in heavenly places – I am there! I am covered with the blood of Christ. Jesus said before the cross *"the prince of this world comes and has **nothing** in me"* (John 14:30) – no ground, no place – **nothing**.

When I plead the blood of Christ, what happens is that what was true about Christ becomes true about me and you. The devil has no ground or place in you – that's our high ground and that's our refuge and our stronghold. Not our own strength, not our own wits, not our own knowledge, not even our own faith. Our high ground is the blood of Christ.

3. Our high ground is our covenantal relationships in the Body of Christ.

You and I are part of the Body of Christ. Let me explain how this works. Imagine that you are in a church with many other believers and holding hands along the rows and across the gangways. Now if someone comes into the room and tries to take hold of just one of those believers there, he is going to have a

24

problem. As the intruder tries to pull a person out, so he confronts all the strength of the whole Body there, because all are joined (holding hands) with one another. He is going to have a problem! This simple illustration shows that we are locked into the Body of Christ by covenant, bound into a covenantal relationship with the entire Body of Christ, not just in our local village or town but right across the world. Millions and millions of Christians are involved.

In the past and in the ages to come there is a "great crowd of witnesses." You and I are locked together into that Body. That is our high place – our place of security.

We need to know not only what that high place is, but we also need to know how to get into it. Do you know how to step into that high place within yourself? You must proclaim that 'I am seated in heavenly places in Christ Jesus. My life is hid with Christ in God. I am covered by the blood of the cross. The devil has nothing in me. I am part of the Body of Christ and Christ is my Head.'

You need to know how to step back onto this high ground. You also need to learn to do it before you **have** to do it. This should be part of our daily training because when you need to do it may be too late. You get up tomorrow morning feeling fine, rejoicing in God and ready to face another day then suddenly, a short while later, "the sky falls in on your head!" It is too late then to think "I've got the high ground somewhere. What was the high ground? I am sure Tom Marshall told me what it was!"

We need to know beforehand so that we are prepared for the attack. We should practise that – *"God **trains** our hands for war."* We must **train** to defend ourselves. On every occasion, under every pressure, through every trial and in everything that happens to us, we have got to know where our high ground is and learn how to get on to it. I think that this should be part of the daily exercise of believers in these days.

Every commanding officer spends an enormous amount of time training troops before he sends them into the trenches! We know that there is a war, but we can't just say, as many Christians do, "let's go and have a charge at the enemy somewhere." Often we Christians are an untrained bundle of troops thrust into the battlefield in total disarray and we then wonder why we have problems.

When you are occupying the high ground you can see what is going on. You get above the smoke of battle, above the din and above the confusion. One of the things that distinguishes a trainee exercise by the Holy Spirit, and a spiritual attack is clear and obvious. God says "face this, go through this, this will be good for you" if you are listening to what he is saying. The mark of a spiritual attack so often is chaos and confusion and you don't understand what is going on. You are attacked from behind – it's bewildering. That is often the mark of a spiritual battle. How are you going to handle that? Get into the high place. From there you can see what is going on much more clearly. You can discern the hand of the devil, the direction of the attack and you can find that place of security – the place of your resources. It is from that place you can say to the devil 'well I am actually hidden with Christ in God if you want me – I am up here. I am covered by the blood of Christ. If you attack me you actually attack the whole of the Body of Christ because I am part of this Body.' You must learn to do this.

Primary rules:

1. With every pressure on your patience, step back into the Body of Christ, into your high place. Every stress you come under, step back into your high place. Learn to do it, learn to get there, learn to be there. This is a primary rule.

2. Build an effective defensive system and learn how to defend yourself. What does this mean?

    a) Develop an attitude of confidence. Deal with the question of fear. You need to have a fear-free defence system. Fear saps our morale. Fear confuses us. Fear makes us react in the wrong way. Where is this attitude of confidence to come from? By seeing things the way they really are.
    Remember how Elisha was in the town of Dothan one time and the armies of the Assyrians were round the hills outside of the city? Elisha's servant was terrified. What did Elisha do? He

asked God to open his eyes. I think Elisha was half humorous about that because he could see things the young fellow couldn't see. The Lord then opened the servant's eyes and he saw: *"those who are for us are more than those who are against us"* (2 Kings 6:16). When we see reality, when we see that God is on our side and he is for us, who can be against us?

Do you know what it means that you are filled with the Holy Spirit? The Holy Spirit is God localised in your body. It's a wonderful thought. The Holy Spirit is omnipotent God, omniscient God, eternal God, localised in your human body. This body is the temple of the Holy Spirit. Therefore if God eternal, omnipotent and omniscient is in you, to say that "he that is for us is more than those that are against us" is the understatement of the century! The Bible also says, that *"greater is he that is in you that he that is in the world"* (1 John 4:4). We must therefore build our defence system by getting our confidence right.

Confidence is trust that has been proved right so often that you don't need to think about it. David had trusted God so often and proved God so much that he said that *"though war break out against me, even then **will I be confident.**"* (Psalm 27:3).

I find that a lot of Christians today are not confident. They are desperately struggling to trust God and to have more faith. They need to learn to have a place of confidence. Do you know God? God's character never changes. You can be confident in that. God's Word never changes. You can be confident in that as well. Have you ever thought what would happen if you went to the Lord believing one of his promises and you heard him say, "I am sorry, I have changed my mind. It doesn't apply any more." It's unthinkable. God keeps his Word. When God makes a promise to us he limits his Sovereignty for all eternity. God limits his freedom of action for ever. There are some things that God literally can not do. Why? Because He has promised otherwise. He takes promises very seriously.

Do you know why we may have problems with faith? Basically it is because we are faithless people. We make promises very lightly these days and we break them with very little compunction. Most promises we make have got an unwritten proviso I have discovered. It is this – "as long as I still feel the same," "as long as I discover that I have not made a mistake," "as long as something more important doesn't turn up," "as long as it doesn't cost too much," I promise. Remember that God's promises are not conditional. Once he has promised that's it. If I want to grow in faith I must start taking God's promises seriously. One of the reasons we have difficulty in believing God is because if **we** take promises lightly, we find it difficult to believe that anybody else, particularly God, will take them seriously.

b) Clear away entanglements. Get rid of things that endanger you spiritually. It is very difficult to fight somebody with your shoelaces tied and with your feet entangled!

The devil tries to entangle us because that inhibits our freedom of action when we come to defending ourselves. Because we are in a war the war has to take priority. I believe that God's people these days have to take this matter seriously and get rid of entanglements.

What do I mean by this? For some people they are relational entanglements. Some relationships you have may be of no help to you and even a potential danger to you – they somehow inhibit your freedom of action. They must go.

Sometimes it is financial entanglements. Freedom of action for many people is severely limited because of these. If possible get free of such. Be rid of them.

Sometimes it is habits – debilitating habits that sap our spiritual energies. Sometimes this is a particular danger for leaders who are involved in so many activities – some of which are none of their business! These just sap energy and distract us from our main task. We need to have a sharp focus as to what God means us to be involved in.

Summary

Note the extreme importance of defence. Lack of secure defences leave us open to surprise attack.

The devil will often try to rush our defences and catch us unprepared.

1. Occupy the High Ground (Psalm 91), where you have protection (vs 1-2), are in touch with resources of divine power (vs 3-7), and can discern what is going on (v8).

Note David's reliance on the high ground. (Psalm 18:2-3, 16-19, 27:5; 61:2-3). Our high ground is:

a. Our position and standing in Christ – (Ephesians 2:6, 1:18-23; Colossians 3:1-4).

b. The victory of the Cross and Resurrection – (Colossians 2:15; Hebrews 2:14; Revelation 12:11).

c. Our covenant relationship with God – (Hebrews 6:17-18).

Satan will always try to draw us off our high ground on to his.

2. Build an Effective Defence System before it is needed. (Psalm 144:1; 18:34).

a. Develop an attitude of confidence – (Psalm 27:1-3; Jeremiah 17:7). Deal with fear, be confident in the Cross, be confident in the Holy Spirit, and be confident in the Word of God. God's counsel brings to nothing the purposes of the enemy. (Isaiah 8:9-10; Proverbs 21:30-31).

b. Clear away entanglements that hinder our effectiveness or make us vulnerable. These entanglements may include relationships, finances, debilitating habits or energy-draining thought patterns, complicated and non-productive activities, and issues and situations that are not our business. (2 Corinthians 6:14; 1 Timothy 6:9-10; Matthew 6:25-34; Hebrews 2:1).

5

Understanding the
Armour of God

Ephesians 6 tells us to *"put on the full armour of God."* For a long time that passage never meant a great deal to me. I have friends who religiously get up each day and put on their helmet of salvation, their breastplate and tighten their belt, and get their shield and sword and go off to the office. I tried to imagine that and it wasn't an awful lot of help to me. However one day I started to understand what the armour of God is. This is very important.

The armour of God is a set of life conditions that God wants to establish in you. And when these are established they enable God to work and they prevent Satan from working. The word panoplia meaning full-armour, is used in the New Testament – once in Ephesians 6 and once in Luke 11 where Jesus is talking about the devil. He says *"when a strong man fully armed keeps his household everything is at peace."*

Jesus is saying that God has got a full armour, and the devil has a full armour. What is the latter? It is a set of life conditions that he wants to establish in your life. And when they take root in your life they enable him to work, and they prohibit God from working.

As far as warfare is concerned the life conditions in Ephesians 6 are the critical ones. There are other conditions that are important for your maturity, your growth and so on, but as far as defence is concerned Ephesians 6 names the critical ones. What are they?

God's Life Conditions

1. Truth
Husbands and wives need to walk in the light with one another, speaking the truth to one another. All the truth. Anything that is

hidden from one another is a potential danger.

Brothers and sisters in the Body of Christ need to learn to walk in the light with one another. In the eldership of the church I came from in New Zealand we had come to a very wonderful place of truth-speaking amongst the brethren, to the extent that if one of them said something I knew they meant exactly what those words said. There was no hidden agenda. I could trust them. I could say just what I wanted to say, I didn't have to dress it up in any kind of way or say it obliquely so that they would take the right inference out of it. I could just say it and I knew that they would take it at face value. However, it took us so long and there was so much pain to get to that place, I realised just how little truth-speaking had been going on amongst us. We don't say it the way it is. It sometimes hurts to walk in the truth but truth is a wonderful thing.

Sometimes truth wounds, but this wounding heals very quickly. The safest place to be is in the light. Why? Because the devil hates the light. The devil does not come to the light. Jesus said *"whoever comes to the light his deeds are discovered"* (John 3:21). This means judgement on sin, and on wickedness. Walking in the light is the safest place to be. Get that established in your life.

2. Peace (Shalom)

Let me tell you something interesting about peace. Peace to the Hebrews was not the absence of war. Peace to the Hebrews was harmony with your friends and victory over your enemies. Isn't that interesting? That's shalom. Now I understand what Paul meant when he said *"Now the God of peace, the God of Shalom, will bruise Satan under your feet"* (Romans 16:20). That doesn't sound a very peaceful thing, does it? But it is.

Let God establish harmony in your life with your friends and victory over your enemies, peace with God over your sin, peace with God over his dealings in your life and, more than that, the peace of God that garrisons our hearts and minds.

3. Faith – Trust

Let me tell you some important things about trust. Trust is a choice you make. It is a risk you take. There is no such thing as costless, riskless trust. The risk you take is that you let the outcome of some part of your life go out of your hands into somebody else's hands. The risk, therefore, in trusting God is that we let some of the outcome of lives go out of our control, into his. It doesn't surprise me that we are supposed to trust God but it does surprise me that God trusts us. God lives by the terms of his own relationships. In other words God trusts us and trust is a choice God makes, and trust is a risk God takes. Amazing. God takes risks with us! He lets some of the outcome of his purposes go out of his hands into ours. That's awesome. When Jesus went back to heaven and left all the destiny of his kingdom in the hands of eleven apostles he actually did not have a backup second 'team' waiting in the wings if the first lot failed. He trusted us to preach the Gospel to every creature.

4. Hope – The helmet of Salvation

Hope is one of the most neglected virtues in the whole of our Christian calendar. Paul says in Corinthians chapter 13, *"now abide faith, hope, love, these three and the greatest of these is love."* In my lifetime I have heard hundreds of sermons on love, hundreds of sermons on faith but only two preached on hope – and I preached both! What has happened to hope?

Let me give you a definition of hope – this wonderful thing. In the Bible hope is the confident expectation of something good. In other words hope is the openness to receive. You will not experience what you don't receive. If you don't receive the love of God you won't experience it. If you don't receive the blessing of God you won't experience it. Nobody experiences more than they receive but you will not receive more than you are open to. If you are not open to healing you won't receive it. If you are not open to encouragement you won't receive it. God's problem is not in the giving because it is his nature to give. God's problem is getting us to receive, and hope is the openness to receive.

We ought to be the most open people on the face of the earth. Do you know what despair is in the Bible? A despairing person is a person whose future has closed in on themselves. No way out – that's despair. No future. Hope, however, is the opposite. All Christians ought to be 'open' people, open to God, open to one another, open to life, open to everything apart from sin. Hope is wonderful.

The devil's life conditions are the reverse of God's life conditions.

> *The armour of God is truth – the devil's is deception and lies.*
> *The armour of God is peace – the devil's is strife and contention.*
> *The armour of God is hope – the devil's is despair and depression.*
> *The armour of God is faith – the devil's is mistrust and suspicion.*

We need to understand and take on board the life conditions that God wants to establish in us and work on them every day. Why? Because once they are established they become our armour. They become our protection. Understand the armour of God.

Summary

The armour of God is a set of **life conditions** God wants to establish in our life, to enable him to work, and to prevent Satan from working (Cf Luke 11:21).

Truth – The effect of truth is to expose lies and so protect us from the devil's deception. (Ephesians 6:14; 2 Corinthians 6:7; John 3:19-20).

Righteousness – Our covenant relationship with God through Christ that guarantees safety and ensures victory – (Isaiah 59:17; 2 Corinthians 6:7).

Peace (shalom) – harmony with our friends and victory over our enemies (Romans 16:20). Not only peace with God but the peace of God to guard our hearts and minds (Philippians 4:7; Colossians 3:15).

Faith – The creative link that enables God's power to be shared with man (1 John 5:4; Ephesians 6:16).

Hope – the confident expectation of something good – the openness to receive (Hosea 2:15).

Love that not only links us to the life of God but is the life of God (1 John 5:2-5; 2 Corinthians 6:6).

The Word of God – The rhema, revelatory word through the Spirit (Ephesians 6:17; Hebrews 1:3; 1 Peter 1:25).

Prayer in the Spirit – (Ephesians 6:18, Jude 20).

6

Examine your Resources

It is vital for all of us in the battle to examine our resources and to know what they are. Do you know what yours are?

1. Your resources are your strengths, the things you do well.
Be honest. Spiritually, what are the things that you do really well? If you say you do nothing really well, that is the devil lying to you. What are you good at? For example, I am good at praising God when I am feeling gloomy – that's a strength. I can believe God for healing my body – that's a strength. I can encourage people who are down – that's a strength.

Understand that God has given you two sets of things. Firstly, strengths, gifts and things you are good at doing. Secondly, limitations. Limitations are in your life to make room for other people. If you had all the strengths you need, you wouldn't need anybody else. You would be self-sufficient. God has made you with limitations.

Because of our fallenness we also have weaknesses. Weaknesses you can overcome and you are supposed to overcome, but limitations you will never overcome. God made you with these to be good at some things but not good at everything. The limitations in your life make room for other people and your strengths help somebody else's limitations. Remember, however, that you must know what your strengths are and use them as part of your resources.

2. Your resources are the Body of Christ.
Let me point something out to you and explain what I mean. Think of a church with, say, three hundred people in the congregation. Probably over half of these have been Christians for more than

10 years, a quarter for more than 5 years and the rest, say, about 2 years. If you look at this as an average it would be fair to guess at this being about 7 years. Now with a congregation of this size you therefore have access to approximately 2,100 years of spiritual experience! It is therefore unlikely that you would come across many circumstances in life that had not been faced and overcome by someone in this congregation. These are your resources to call upon. You should be able to find at least one person that has suffered or gone through a trial similar to yours within that congregation.

3. Your resources are the relationships you can depend on.
They too are our strengths. People who are living in friendship and covenant with you are those that you should be able to ring up at any time of the day or night to ask them to pray with or for you. If you have a problem you can call on them and they will be sure to help. If I am facing trouble or attack from a situation they will stand with me. Those are my important relationships and those are my resources in the Body of Christ.

It is vitally important to have these and to have people who are loyal to us and to whom we can be loyal. Do you know what loyalty is?

Loyalty says, 'I will be with you in the bad times as well as the good.' We talk about a fairweather friend – that's a 'friend' who is only there in the good times. Our true friends are there in the bad times as well.

Loyalty says I will be for you even if everybody else is against you.

Loyalty says I will defend you even at risk or cost to myself.

We need loyal friends. We need relationships that will stand the strain, and stand extraordinary strain if need be. Such people are to be prized almost above anything else. A proverb says *"A brother is born for adversity"* (Proverbs 17:17). Friends are born for adversity, to stick with you through thick and thin. Such friends are much rarer than they ought to be.

I remember a friend of mine in America who grew up amongst the street gangs in his younger days. He said to me once that if he was in a real tight spot he would rather have some of the guys out of the gang at his back than some of his ministerial colleagues! They would run for cover, but that gang was dependable.

You not only need loyal friends but you also need to know who they are. This friendship has to be cultivated before it is needed. You need to know how much strain your friendship will take because if you overload a relationship with more than it can take you will probably damage both friendship and friend.

Summary

Examine your Resources
You cannot fight in someone else's armour (1 Samuel 17:38-40). Assess your personal life and experience to discover:

a. **Your spiritual strengths** – the things you do well. Your perseverance, patience, hopefulness, good response to pressure, discernment, etc.

b. **The things you really know** – have confidence in what you know, in revelation truth and what you have proved in your experience, the rhema word.

c. **Relationships you can depend on in difficult times,** and those you trust and can work effectively with.

d. **The Body of Christ** – the faith, experience and knowledge available in the Christian community you belong to.

7

Learn to Handle
Spiritual Pressure

We all know that we have to live in a real world where there are
real anxieties and real stresses. All of us are regularly under stress
of one kind or another. So often we can sing victory songs in
church, but how do you feel the next morning when you go to
work? Be honest. I expect that you feel totally powerless for most
of the time. Isn't that right?

We need to understand that God knows all about that. We are in
fact to find our destiny on the battlefield. The battlefield is for our
good. He is maturing the saints through the pain barrier.

I remember some time ago speaking to a young woman who
was telling me how she had just finished her first marathon race.
She had run 42 kilometres. She explained to me that when you are
running a marathon, around the 24 kilometre mark you hit what is
called the pain barrier. When you hit this one of two things
happen. Either you body gives up and you die by the side of the
road, or you struggle through the pain and you know that even if
you don't win, you are somehow going to finish the race. Now
when she said that, I realised that all around our lives there are
these pain barriers. Not all the unpleasant stressful things that
happen to us are bad for us. Most of them are actually necessary
to us. They are, if you like, growing pains. For example, you
cannot grow physically without hitting the pain barrier. If you
want to strengthen your arms you lift weights until your arms are
ready to drop – then you start lifting more weights! Or you may
want to develop stamina, so you go jogging, and just when you
are about to collapse – you jog some more!

You can't grow intellectually without the pain barrier.
Everybody who has studied understands that. It hurts to concentrate
and try and understand enough to take notes and then it hurts to

41

try and remember what you are meant to have learned! It's a pain barrier.

You can't grow relationally without the pain barrier. You hurt people and they hurt you. It hurts to apologise and ask for forgiveness and then start all over again.

You can't grow spiritually without the pain barrier. One of the interesting things about God is that he is very honest. He never says "this is going to hurt me more than it hurts you". He says "this is going to hurt you" but afterwards, if you are exercised by it, you get the peaceful fruits of righteousness.

What I want to emphasise is that you can't ever avoid pain. If you don't get the pain of exercise you get the pain of a sick body. If you don't go through the pain of study you get the pain of ignorance. If you don't go through the pain of relationships you get the pain of loneliness. You can't avoid pain so you might as well make it productive.

Some of the pain and struggle that we go through in our lives are part of the exercise that the Holy Spirit is putting in our way to build spiritual stamina and muscle into us.

But not all pain is of that kind. Sometimes it will be an attack by the devil on your position, on your life, and on your health, and we need to know how to handle that. There will be the day when all of us find ourselves in the middle of a war that is not of our making. It was here before ever you and I were on the scene. It is a real war. It is not a metaphorical war. It is not a make-believe war. It is the aim of Satan to separate God from his creation Word. Do you know what his creation Word is? It is two things. Firstly God said *"let us make man in our image after our likeness and let them have dominion"* (Genesis 1:26). That is God's declared purpose. Secondly he said *"the whole earth will be filled with the glory of God as the waters cover the sea."* Satan's attempt is to separate God from that Word.

Use every experience of spiritual pressure as a learning process. Under pressure always fall back onto what you know. What you know is your armour. You can't fall back onto somebody else's knowledge. You can't fight wearing somebody else's armour – David discovered that with Saul before tackling Goliath! You can only fight in your own armour. Your armour is what you know.

Under pressure we always retreat to what we know and the greater the pressure is, the more fundamental becomes that retreat. I say this because I can remember a time in my life when I had my back spiritually right up 'against a wall'. All that I was left with was this statement of just three words from Psalm 23 – *'The Lord Is!'* Wonderful! *The Lord Is.* That saved me. That saved my sanity. Everything else had gone but I fell back into the refuge, into the strong tower. Nothing could change the fact that *The Lord Is.*

The more pressure there is, the more basic will be the thing you fall back onto. You go back beyond your faith. Paul lived through enormously difficult circumstances but he dug himself right down to that bedrock. Paul knew that. He was who he was, where he was, because ultimately God had purposed it. He knew the *"purpose of Him who works all things according to the counsel of his will."* That is the fundamental thing – that's the ultimate thing.

Learn how to handle spiritual pressure in every circumstance. Remember you have got to train and practise defence until it becomes instinctive. Don't think, "I can't manage this." No, use the circumstance as an exercise to step back into the high place. Do this until it becomes habitual, until the instinctive thing under any pressure is to go back onto the high ground and to your place of security. It is when you learn to do this that you can handle situations of attack from the devil.

I believe that what I have endeavoured to convey to you will be of fundamental importance to Christians in the days to come.

Defence is only the preliminary. In this booklet I have emphasised that you have got to first learn to defend yourself before you can attack. So many Christians get this the wrong way round and are surprised when they meet defeat.

Finally you will see that in Psalm 18 and verse 28 it says,

> *"You O Lord, keep my lamp burning,*
> *My God turns my darkness into light."*

(David was in his high place seeing what was going on).

> *"With your help I can advance against a troop,*
> *With my God I can scale a wall."*   (Verse 29).

From your defence, you can now mount an offence.

Summary

Spiritual pressure rarely sends advance warnings, so we need to know the nature of our high ground and how to reach it. We need to understand the different pains and stresses in our life; and how to fall back instinctively and automatically into a secure place without having to stop and think about it. Our defence must become second nature to us, and we must use every occasion to practise it.

8

In
Conclusion

Identify the true source of the attack

People are never the enemy, although the attack may often come through people. (Ephesians 6:12; Matthew 16:23).

Discern the nature of the attack and the devil's strategy

a. It will generally be directed towards an area of weakness, (Ephesians 4:27), or an area of ignorance (2 Corinthians 2:10-11).

b. Watch out for any negative, compulsive reactions and responses, and shut them down. Our victory is in Christ, but preparation and composure are our responsibility.

Be confident

You cannot win with a loser's expectancy, or if you feel 'unworthy'. The principle of victory is still *"according to your faith be it unto you."* Resolve that you will not quit but will win (Romans 8:37). We are more than conquerors.

Stand fast and resist the attack

a. It takes energy for demons to attack. A simple resolute refusal to yield based on our position in Christ, will sap the enemy's strength.

b. When we stand fast, what the devil dreads is the possibility of Christ's intervention on our behalf, (James 4:7-8; 1 Peter 5:8-10).

c. Attack the devil's attack, and make use of: intercession to thwart the enemy's plans (Psalm 33:10; Isaiah 8:7-11): praise and worship to confound his powers, (2 Chronicles 20:21; Psalm 149:6), and the prophetic Scriptures to bind the enemy, (Revelation 12:11; Matthew 16:19).

Recognise the occasions when confrontation may not be the right thing to do

There are times when it is wise to duck (1 Samuel 18:7-11). *"A man's wisdom gives him patience; it is to his glory to overlook an offence"* (Proverbs 19:11).

On occasions when we are not ready or we don't know what to do or how to handle the situation, the best thing to do might be to withdraw or run away. *"The name of the Lord is a strong tower, the righteous run to it and are safe"* (Proverbs 18:10).

If you have enjoyed this book and would like to help us to send a copy of it and many other titles to needy pastors in the **Third World**, please write for further information or send your gift to:

Sovereign World Trust, P.O. Box 777, Tonbridge, Kent TN11 9XT, United Kingdom

or to the **'Sovereign World'** distributor in your country. If sending money from outside the United Kingdom, please send an International Money Order or Foreign Bank Draft in STERLING, drawn on a **UK** bank to **Sovereign World Trust**.